C000056331

Joerg Marxen

The Value of Longing

Toward a mature perspective

**Lecture given on February 8, 2020
at the symposium
"Alexa – still' meine Sehnsucht"
[Alexa – still my longing]
held from
February 7 – 9, 2020
in Bad Oeynhausen, Germany**

Copyright: © 2020 Joerg Marxen
Editing: Erik Kinting - www.buchlektorat.net
Cover and typesetting: Erik Kinting
Cover photo: © Joerg Marxen
Translator: Alison Mally – www.mally-fachuebersetzungen.de
Publisher: tredition GmbH, Halenreie 40-44, 22359 Hamburg

978-3-347-14839-0 (paperback)
978-3-347-14840-6 (hardcover)
978-3-347-14841-3 (eBook)

ISBNs of the German edition:
978-3-347-14836-9 (paperback)
978-3-347-14837-6 (hardcover)
978-3-347-14838-3 (eBook)

The symposium entitled *Alexa – still' meine Sehnsucht* [Alexa – still my longing] was organized by *Median Klinik* am Park Bad Oeynhausen in conjunction with the *Weiterbildungskreis Psychosomatische Medizin und Analytische Psychotherapie e. V.* and the *Psychotherapeutisches Lehrinstitut ZAP GmbH*, a state-approved training center for psychological psychotherapists and child and youth psychotherapists.

Joerg Marxen is a registered psychological psychotherapist and coach (depth psychology, hypnotherapy, value system analysis and corporate development theory).

Author:
Joerg Marxen
Am Neuen Petritore 7
38100 Braunschweig
Germany
joerg.marxen@marxen.org

Foreword

In 2011, the American Psychological Association published an article entitled "Is Longing Only for Germans? A Cross-Cultural Comparison of *Sehnsucht* in Germany and the United States". The authors (Scheibe, Blanchard-Fields, Wiest & Freund, 2011) emphasize that despite all the differences longing is of importance in both cultures and can have functional and dysfunctional effects in both cultures.

I have repeatedly witnessed the phenomenon that longing can be an existential blessing for one person and a devastating catastrophe for another. This made me look at the factors that make the difference, that allow us to make beneficial use of phenomena from the field of longing.

Joerg Marxen

Table of Contents

The field of longing

Longing has a function.
Longing springs from a source.
Longing has an effect.
Longing can have a very destructive effect.
Longing can, however, also have an exceptionally constructive effect.

Longing and how we deal with it are in play as an effect but also as a cause, for example when relationships fall apart or when relationships, our attitude to life, our capacity for pleasure and our performance capability develop more favorably or less favorably. They are in play when a happy couple is expecting a child and then during the pregnancy or after the birth of the child the partner falls in love with another woman, or at least begins a sexual relationship with someone else. Longing can lead us into new situations against, through or even despite great reservations, in which we encounter new people and new challenges and in which we first have to reorient ourselves.

In the field of *religiosity, spirituality and transcendence*, too, it is usually very much about longing and how we deal it.

Longing constantly affects our lives in many areas.

The German dictionary of the Brothers Grimm (1971) devotes a long paragraph to the phenomenon of longing [German: *Sehnsucht*] and its facets with numerous statements, one of which is that we can understand longing as being ...

> ... a high degree of intense and often painful desire for something, particularly if there is no hope of attaining what is desired, or when its attainment is uncertain, still far away.

Dictionary of the Brothers Grimm
(Grimm, J. & Grimm, W., 1971)

This quote is also used by the *Sehnsucht* researchers surrounding Paul Baltes, Alexandra Freund and Susanne Scheibe (Scheibe et al., 2007), who start from a developmental perspective of the entire life span and whose definition and characterization I essentially follow.

They characterize the phenomenon of life longings with the aid of six criteria:
1. their unrealizability
2. a sense of incompleteness and imperfection in one's own life

3. a tritime focus
4. the accompanying phenomenon of bitter-sweet or sweet-bitter feelings
5. the observation that life longings invite one to look back and evaluate life and life options
6. and their symbolic character and symbolic richness.

They define their understanding as follows:

The first two characteristics go hand in hand; on the one side, the thoughts, desires and emotions associated with personal utopias or the search for an optimal life and on the other hand, the accompanying sense of incompleteness and imperfection in life. Together, these two aspects generate the bitter sweetness or sweet bitterness of life longings, the combination of desire and disappointment and the search for ways to deal with this conflict.

Longing can help us to develop vision. In the feelings of well-being that arise when we imagine our dreams materializing, its quality of sweetness becomes apparent.

By contrast, it can be bitter when we realize that what we long for, what seems like the fulfilment of our dreams, is not fully attainable, is not attainable in the foreseeable future, or indeed at all, and turns out to be permanently unattainable.

A tritime focus does not mean that the entire life span from childhood to the present and into old age is necessarily always considered and borne in mind. However, it is assumed that the feeling of longing always extends from the present moment back into the past as well as forward into the future.

Given this background and often laden with ambivalent feelings, longing can cause us again and again to look back on the life we have lived and can follow us, prompting us to evaluate what is harmonious and fulfilling, what has been successful and what we still have to learn.

Another essential characteristic is the wealth of symbolic meaning. If we keep the symbolic richness in mind, we see that longings are much more than a specific type of behavior or experience. We see that the specific objects or goals of longings are connected to broader mental and emotional representations of what they stand for. We peer into a large, wide space behind them, or at least have an inkling of that space.

According to this characteristic of longing, a specific desire or yearning, for example for a hug from someone you love, is not necessarily a manifestation of longing. According to Baltes, a wish is only seen as a manifestation of longing when the mental and emotional representations associated with it are connected behind it with a larger construct of thoughts and feelings about the direction of one's own life. Seen in this light, the desire for a hug could of course be only a mundane wish but behind this could also be the longing for intimacy in general.

So far for the findings provided by the researchers surrounding Paul Baltes (cf. Scheibe et al., 2007).

The compass function of longing

In the interaction of these characteristics, especially the tritime focus and life evaluation, longing has a compass function:

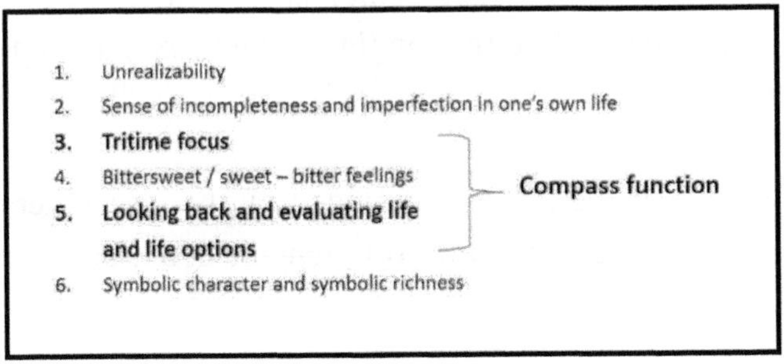

1. Unrealizability
2. Sense of incompleteness and imperfection in one's own life
3. **Tritime focus**
4. Bittersweet / sweet – bitter feelings — } **Compass function**
5. **Looking back and evaluating life and life options**
6. Symbolic character and symbolic richness

Figure 1 Compass function of longing

With the aid of this compass function, we can, for example, look back and question to what extent we have been true to ourselves in the past. We can question how much we agree with how we shape our present life and we can allow the compass effect of longing to question us about how we should direct our life in the future, how we can best be true to ourselves in the interplay of that which yearns for development and that which demands acceptance of the realities of our life.

The unattainability of longing

The literature on longing uses the term *unattainability* sometimes when it is not a question of an endless waiting time but only a very long waiting time until fulfilment. But since a clear distinction at this exact point of the definition can make all the difference between happiness and unhappiness, I assume that whatever can be achieved on any occasion is never the longing itself.

If it is attainable,
it is not the longing itself.

I will show why this is perhaps an uncomfortable thought at first, but which ultimately liberates us, makes us more professional and helps us to deal more confidently and constructively with our own life and with the demands on our role as therapists, in the latter case especially when dealing with transference and countertransference. I will also demonstrate why it creates the conditions for being able to experience a certain quality of longing that is not always immediately recognizable as such.

We can long for love, power, success, identity, social connectedness, possibly also for religiosity, spirituality and transcendence.

All these longings can be present in various aggregate states:

- they may be consciously accessible to us;
- they may be present but not yet developed, or
- they may be rejected.

Regardless of the form they take, they can pose an exceptional challenge to us when dealing with our own longing as well as when we are the therapist, friend or companion of a person to whom they are currently being revealed.

The struggle for maturity

At times, parents experience this challenge as if they were being tested on how mature they are when responding to their children.

A positive example of this:
A party with friends; adults and children in a relaxed and cheerful atmosphere. At some point it is time to go home with one's child. He's overexcited and he's angry that he has to leave. On the way home through a quiet village late in the evening, he loudly announces for all the inquisitive neighbors to hear how cruel and horrible he thinks his parents are because he has to go home so early. The parents remain calm but firm. A quarter of an hour later the child is beaming happily and falls asleep quickly and blissfully.
The parents have set limits for the child and given him direction. Repeatedly and whenever necessary, in this and in similar situations.

Banal? Perhaps. Twenty-five years later, this same child says that at times it was precisely situations such as these that gave him a lot of strength for the difficult moments in his life, a feeling of being safe and secure with whatever life may bring, even if he is experiencing intense, unhappy sensations or is facing what at first glance seem to be insuperable challenges or conflicts.

Something is becoming apparent, i.e. something is "shining through" here. According to the definition of the research group surrounding Baltes (Scheibe et al., 2007), the parents have evidently not only responded to a child's situational need for limits, but also to a fundamental underlying longing to be heard and be given an unconditional and reliable feeling of security.

In the example above, setting limits in a loving manner was a mature, healthy response on the part of the parents to an obvious longing for a response to a present need, a response that had a lasting positive effect. In each of these situations, the parents were perhaps not even aware that they were not only responding to a situational need but also to a deep underlying longing.

It does not always end as well when we are challenged by powerfully charged symbols of longing, at least not at the first attempt.

Here is another example:

A person from a poor background rises in the world until he is living in circumstances that are exceptionally pleasant from a material point of view and he has attained an enviable social and professional position. Then, in a flash he loses everything and finds himself back in the poor situation he was in at the beginning. His subjective experience tells him that he will now stay there forever.

This is precisely what happens to the person who is symbolically represented by two people in the fairy tale of the fisherman and his wife by the Grimm Brothers (cf. Grimm, J., W. & Laimgruber, M. (1978): *Vom Fischer und seiner Frau,* Artemis).
If we place the emphasis of the interpretation not on a relationship dynamic between two people (which would of course be possible), but rather on the representation of an intrapersonal dynamic, then one of the parts of the personality of our protagonist enters the stage of the fairy tale as a fisherman and one as the fisherman's wife.
The fisherman saves the life of an enchanted prince who has been turned into a fish that is swimming in a pond. In return, the prince is able and willing to grant the fisherman his wishes. The wife of the fisherman insists on relentlessly exploiting this resource. On his wife's insistence, virtually at her

mercy, the fisherman passes on her insatiable wishes to the fish, albeit with misgivings.

As symbols for the wishes, and through their initial fulfilment at first also for the triumphs of the protagonist, the fairy tale cites the move from a small hut to a cottage, the move to a castle and becoming king, emperor and finally pope.

The part of the personality symbolized by the woman is obviously able to feel deep longing and passion and makes unreasonable and outrageous demands.

The other internal figure, the fisherman, would like to observe the limits of what is possible and appropriate, he senses his own impulse not to make immoderate demands, to know when enough is enough, to know when to be humble.

The quality of immaturity is inherent in both figures; their joint action is not yet coordinated or coherent action.

Without his intensely felt longing, this person would never have had the courage and drive to challenge and use his resources, although still immature, to improve his situation. Nothing would have changed. There would have been no moving into a house, into a palace, no development from king to emperor to pope.

What if we could intervene at this point? What would have happened if the person whose destiny unfolds before our eyes had had a good therapist, sufficiently positive transference and trust, what if he had worked on the symbols of his conflict and had exercised self-restraint?

What if the part of the personality symbolized by the fisherman had succeeded in restraining the part of the personality represented by the woman, with respect for its qualities, at this stage of development at the latest?

It probably would not have turned out to be such a moving tale.

However, there is no restraint. The fisherman tells the fish that his wife wants to become like God. The result of course is that they lose everything. Our protagonist finally ends up back in the fishing hut he started out from. We are given to understand that that is where he sits even today, i.e. for what seems to be for a long time, for what feels like an eternity.

If he had been more humble, the story could perhaps have ended with the person stopping to take stock, at the latest where the pope, as a symbol of the quality of what has been achieved, i.e. an extremely powerful but still human figure, comes into play, as a metaphor for someone who is in contact with the Almighty but is not identified with him.

To do so, he would have had to recognize the desire to be omnipotent as something that is actually unrealizable and must remain so in human terms, as a symbol of an underlying, unrealizable longing.

Without reasonable restraint through rational thinking, it is possible that longing will destroy what has been attained through excessiveness and will transform something which was attainable only a moment ago into something unattainable.

So no matter how the story unfolds, in the end, man is confronted with the fact that the longing behind the symbols, in the present case also the illusionary nature of the symbol for the fantasy of omnipotence, is unattainable, sometimes in a more comfortable situation that makes it easier for him to achieve internal and external objectives, sometimes with more hardship.

If we as human beings want to exploit the value of longing, this can only work in balance with the value of prudence.

C. G. Jung points out that archetypal forces do not necessarily show themselves to be moderate and reasonable, for example when they break into our lives accompanied by deep longing. He emphasizes the importance of the ego dealing with the phenomena that can be experienced as divine powers on an equal footing.

ough
ngth, he
ces and seek

...aling with longing i
fold and have a beneficia
an art. On the one hand,
lowing the longing to ful
plans and habits and lead
sometimes by our making ra
other hand, it can be destruc
ourselves blindly to it.
Longing could also be underst
outcome of a complicated algorith
account a vast number of factors
sciousness cannot oversee and then t
tions. These suggestions can be ingen
ing, frightening or completely unrealist
rational thinking, a down-to-earth appro
good relationship with so-called *banality* i
direct and limit the sometimes fiercely enthu
indulging manifestations of our longings in
that can be acted out or recognize and declare
to be absolutely unworkable at a given moment
to act accordingly.

The v

The value of longing ...
at the moment of des...
disastrous end could be ...
a supposed end or as a p...
able to bear, if it can ind...
period of desperation when...
with the consequences of the...
If we use our imagination to co...
the subject of the fairy tale had...
tic help in dealing with his longin...
his personality and conflicts betwe...
unable to use this help earlier, that...
his personality was unable to restrain...
earlier anyway, then the damage has be...
person has lost everything he has atta...
nally finds himself empty and dazed in t...
back where he started.

This is exactly what has happened man...
before, and can always happen again, to our ...
and possibly even to us.

The person we are accompanying in our thou...
can count himself lucky if, in these dark times,
therapist is able to recognize and handle his lon...
ing, confidentially and calmly, even though ou...
protagonist himself is still unaware of it, and if the

Longing can be conscious or unconscious, ...
already manifest or still in waiting mode like th...
seeds of a plant slumbering in the desert sand. It can
be hidden under a thick layer of reaction formation
or concealed from our conscious mind by dissocia-
tion.

If the seed in the desert sand does not cry out loud
constantly, this does not mean that it does not carry
a yearning for water. Sometimes the desire for a
certain type of longing only awakens once it finds
an echo and sometimes longings only become apparent in times of great need and in situations we
experience as intolerable and overwhelming.

Why should a mature, successful person who leads
a fulfilling life, who is popular and rooted in a stable circle of friends and colleagues, even remotely
concern himself with the question of how he can
further strengthen the mature parts of his personality or how he can make his internal structure even
more resilient? Wouldn't that be a waste of time?
The question is understandable, but at times a
longing surfaces in a successful life in a symbolic
form that is not immediately comprehensible
without any apparent need and with an intensity far
surpassing anything experienced up until that point.
Or an inexplicable distress arises and it transpires

that it was a longing that made the person become distressed with the result that ultimately the distress and the longing demand a response.

This can take a dramatic turn and even go badly wrong. But it can lead to developmental leaps that were previously inconceivable.

If the guidance provided in such a crisis has been successful, a remarkable phenomenon can be observed with people who have been stable and successful for decades but who have suddenly experienced an extremely intense flood of longing, great stress and a dangerous threat to their stability, namely a touching need to balance two categories of longing, with deep respect for the forces involved.

The criteria provided by the group surrounding Paul Baltes (Scheibe et al., 2007) help to recognize and put into words that in a situation like this something profound and fundamental is emerging and shining through and is also given a name, something that has to do with basic longings and goes far beyond simply meeting current needs.

Such observations and experiences lead me to assume that besides the longing to feel yearning, there are actually two other, existentially significant longings (see Figure 2):

1. a longing for prudence, in the sense of a benevolent, sincere detachment that is strong enough to remain well connected with one's own empathy and compassion yet at the same time stay clearly detached from how these would have us automatically react;
2. and a longing for a lively, dynamic, stable, flexible balance between the longing for the feeling of yearning and the longing for prudence and rationality.

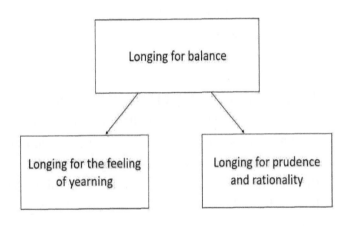

Figure 2 The longing for balance (own figure).

If the longing for balance regulates both forces and creates a healthy interaction, then there is no danger that longing will subdue reason, which at times has terrible, destructive consequences, nor will a dominance of reason crush the longing so that we no longer find any meaning or direction in our lives. We begin to use the value of longing with maturity.

Using the value of longing maturely

There are a multitude of longings that can be communicated to us by our patients' concerns, some of which are from the fields of *religiosity*, *spirituality* and *transcendence*.

Toward the end of his life, Abraham Maslow (1971) found this area of human longings to be of such importance that he included it in his hierarchy of needs in addition to cognitive and aesthetic needs (see Figure 3). This concept of Maslow (1971) and similar references from the works of Graves (1974), Beck and Cowan (1996) as well as Beck and Linscott (1991) suggest two quite different manifestations of spiritual longings:

1. those which at any time, at all stages of development and in any circumstances can permeate people's experiences, and
2. those appearing in highly mature people, that are of such outstanding quality that they have landed at the top of *Maslow's pyramid*.

Figure 3 Extended hierarchy of needs according to Maslow (1971).

Maturity and respect for what we do not understand

What does this mean for our work with people?
It helps, of course, if we have concepts that we can use to reflect on our impressions that help us to recognize patterns and to formulate our *Theory of Mind* about what is going on in our interlocutor.

But fortunately, we do not necessarily need to understand the kind of longing our patients are experiencing. As far as longing is concerned, we are not required to be all-knowing, or be a know-it-all, or to lecture on the longing. Especially if we acknowledge an avowed ignorance in dealing with the longings of our patients, this can provide the space and security they need for their own explorations.

However, even if we have the impression that we do understand or know something of the longings of our patients, then we need to exercise a certain restraint in order to convincingly get across to them that the therapy session is their stage and not ours.

To make this clearer, from 2001 onwards I started to present the dialogue between our patients and ourselves (see appendix) in such a way that they transfer, i.e. communicate, their concerns to us by transference and that we respond to them by countertransference, or rather the way we deal with our countertransference.

> The patient transfers his concern to us through his transference

> We transfer our answer to the patient through our countertransference.

For our answer to be constructive, we remain selectively authentic, are at one with our task and guided by the question of what exactly will best serve the therapeutic process.

The more intense the symbolic and emotional charge of a topic, the more important it is whether and to what extent we are focused on our task, are centered in such a way that we can use our perceptions without being identified with them or without having to relieve tension by acting it out for our own sake.

If we take sides or follow our own agenda, especially when dealing with longing, we might not respond appropriately to our interlocutor but instead burden him with our own issues.

Yet we can also admit to not knowing, and can recall the characteristics of longing and thus create two options:

1. it might be possible to provide a sufficiently secure framework and space in the therapeutic relationship that can be used for the explorations ahead, or
2. we can deal constructively and respectfully with the fact that our patients sometimes create an opportunity to explore particular longings outside the therapeutic process.

It is at this point that the therapist's responsibility ends.

We cannot and do not always need to understand the longing that is communicated to us as the patient's concern. But we are responsible for treating it with due respect and, to the best of our ability, for creating a space for what we initially do not, or indeed will never understand, and even without having to understand the longing in each case, ensuring where necessary that clear boundaries are drawn.

In the God-transference example, no destructive options were conceded to the force of the longing. This subsequently led to insight and enrichment and, due to its compass function, contributed to a meaningful reorientation in life.

Outlook

Longing can appear out of the blue or when a meaningful symbol is lost. Whatever is valuable and precious to us can be lost. Then we grieve for the form. This grieving is sometimes hardly bearable. It may entail a phase of emptiness, all known stages of grief and feelings of desolation. When the longing begins to show a beneficial effect, sometimes an ostensibly undirected move toward searching begins, a revival that is not necessarily accompanied by a keen sense of there being any meaning to it and sometimes even comes with feelings of despair.

But just as Picasso said that inspiration exists, but it has to find us working, the same applies to the compass function of longing: it has to find us in a receptive mode, which can surprisingly sometimes take on the form of an apparently aimless, more or less confused search, which is not recognizable as such.

When new symbols for the longing eventually arise, we consciously experience the compass function of longing, we realize that we are again given a perspective, something that pulls and pushes us, that galvanizes us into action.

If we distinguish between longing and its symbols, if we accept the unrealizability and unattainability of longing, i.e. take it as it is, not as we would like it to be, embrace it as it is, then it rewards us with its hidden quality, with its dependability.

No matter what happens, no matter which symbols of the longing vanish from our lives or turn out to be unattainable, if we allow it, sometimes even if we do not allow it, longing presents us with new symbols, which again, sometimes like a Phoenix after rising from the ashes, points us in a particular direction, gives us a perspective and new goals and the strength to strike out in a new direction.

If *Alexa* could follow the call of the conference topic and had the power to satisfy our longing, we would have to relinquish longing. So perhaps we could consider saying, "Alexa, rescue my longing." But our longing does not need to be rescued. If we are aware of its value and treat it with respect like something valuable, our longing will rescue us.

Bibliography

Sources:

Beck, D. E., & Cowan, C. (1996). *Spiral dynamics: exploring the new science of memetics*. Blackwell Publishers.

Beck, D., & Linscott, G. (1991). *The crucible: Forging South Africa's future*. New Paradigm Press.

Graves, C. W. (1974). Human nature prepares for a momentous leap. *The futurist*, *8*(2), 72–85.

Grimm, J., & Grimm, W. (1971). *Deutsches Wörterbuch*. 16 Bde. in 32 Teilbänden. Leipzig: S. Hirzel 1854–1960.

Grimm, J., Grimm, W., & Laimgruber, M. (1978). *Vom Fischer und seiner Frau*. Artemis.

Maslow, A. H. (1971). *The farther reaches of human nature.* New York, NY, US: Arkana.

Scheibe, S., Freund, A. M., & Baltes, P. B. (2007). Toward a developmental psychology of Sehnsucht (life longings): The optimal (utopian) life. *Developmental psychology*, 43(3), 778.

Scheibe, S., Blanchard-Fields, F., Wiest, M., & Freund, A. M. (2011). Is longing only for Germans? A cross-cultural comparison of Sehnsucht in Germany and the United States. *Developmental psychology*, *47*(3), 603.

Additional literature:

The literature listed here refers to the contents of the lecture and workshop entitled *Die Sehnsucht nach Reife* [The longing for maturity], which was also offered by Joerg Marxen at the symposium *Alexa, still' meine Sehnsucht*.

Adam, K-U. (2003). *Therapeutisches Arbeiten mit dem Ich.* Düsseldorf und Zürich: Walter Verlag.

Altmeyer, M., & Thomä, H. (2010). Einführung: Psychoanalyse und Intersubjektivität. In M. Altmeyer, & H. Thomä (ed.), *Die vernetzte Seele – Die intersubjektive Wende in der Psychoanalyse.* 2. Aufl. Klett-Cotta.

Baltes, P. (2004). *Wisdom as orchestration of mind and virtue.* Book in preparation. http://www.mpib-berlin.mpg.de/en/institut/dok/full/ baltes/orchestr/ [03.03.2020]

Baltes, P. B., & Staudinger, U. M. (2000). Wisdom: A metaheuristic (pragmatic) to orchestrate mind and virtue toward excellence. *American psychologist, 55*(1), 122.

Beck, D. E., Larsen, T. H., Solonin, S., Viljoen, R. C., & Johns, T. Q. (2019). *Spiral Dynamics in der Praxis: Der Mastercode der Menschheit.* J. Kamphausen Verlag.

Bråten, S. (2013). *Roots and collapse of empathy: human nature at its best and at its worst* (Vol. 91). John Benjamins Publishing.

Fikentscher, W. (2004). *Modes of thought: a study in the anthropology of law and religion*. Mohr Siebeck.

Hannah, B. (1985). *Begegnungen mit der Seele: aktive Imagination – der Weg zu Heilung und Ganzheit*. Kösel.

Hermann, S. (1981). Methodik der aktiven Imagination. In U. Eschbach (ed.), *Die Behandlung in der analytischen Psychologie, Band 2. Die Behandlung als menschliche Begegnung*. Fellbach-Oeffingen: Adolf Bonz Verlag.

Hirigoyen, M. F., & Marx, M. (2015). *Die Masken der Niedertracht: seelische Gewalt im Alltag und wie man sich dagegen wehren kann*. Dt. Taschenbuch-Verlag.

Huber, R. (2004). Braucht eine Psychologie Selbsterkenntnis? *Analytische Psychologie, 136, 236–246.*

Hurni, M., & Stoll, G. (1999). *Der Hass auf die Liebe: die Logik der perversen Paarbeziehung*. Psychosozial-Verlag.

Johnson, R. A. (1995). *Bilder der Seele: Traumarbeit und aktive Imagination*. Hugendubel.

Käßmann, M. (2011). *Sehnsucht nach Leben: Mit Bildern von Eberhard Münch*. adeo.

Kast, V. (1988). *Imagination als Raum der Freiheit: Dialog zwischen Ich und Unbewusstem*. Walter-Verlag.

Kast, V. (2012). *Imagination: Zugänge zu inneren Ressourcen finden*. Patmos Verlag.

Küstenmacher, M., Haberer, T., & Küstenmacher, W. T. (2010). *Gott 9.0: wohin unsere Gesellschaft spirituell wachsen wird*. Gütersloher Verlagshaus.

Labek, K., Viviani, R., & Buchheim, A. (2019). Konzeption der Borderline-Persönlichkeitsstörung aus neurobiologischer Sicht. *PTT-Persönlichkeitsstörungen: Theorie und Therapie, 23*(4), 310–320.

Mahr, A. (2016). *Von den Illusionen einer unbeschwerten Kindheit und dem Glück, erwachsen zu sein*. Scorpio Verlag.

Nelles, W. (2012). Umarme Dein Leben. *Wie wir wirklich erwachsen werden*. Köln.

Neumann, E., & Rolfe, E. (1949). *Tiefenpsychologie und neue Ethik*. Depth Psychology and a New Ethic. Zürich: Rascher Verlag.

Pierre, J. C. (2014). *Analyses of Daoism thinking though Clare Graves human development Framework,* Academia.edu

Renggli, F. (2018). *Angst und Geborgenheit: Soziokulturelle Folgen der Mutter-Kind-Beziehung im ersten Lebensjahr*. Rowohlt Verlag GmbH.

Wilkening, F., Freund, A. M., & Martin, M. (2008). *Entwicklungspsychologie*. BeltzPVU.

Zeig, J. K, Munion, W. M. (1999). *Milton H. Erickson*, Sage Publications

Zeig, J. K, 2017). *The Anatomy of Experiential Impact*, Milton H. Erickson Foundation Press

Appendix

Excerpt from the lecture on
Countertransference
on October 24, 2001

by Joerg Marxen
as one of the Wednesday lectures at the *Klinik
Flachsheide* in Bad Salzuflen

(...) By *transference* I mean the totality of all feelings, of all impulses, those that are only perceived and those that are acted out, all acts and omissions, all free expression and all holding back directed from the patient toward the therapist.

Accordingly, I understand *countertransference* to mean the totality of all feelings, impulses, acts, omissions, all free expression and all holding back on the part of the therapist that are directed toward the patient, regardless of whether they have their origin in the patient or, in the Jungian sense, in the field, or in us, whether syntonic or illusionary.

It can happen that besides negative and hard to tolerate qualities in the transference, in the projection, positive values and deep inner qualities might also be projected onto the therapist. All the areas in which the distinction between object and subject has not yet become conscious are initially projected and can become evident in this way and be experienced. When returned to the subject they finally become conscious and integrated.

I propose defining the process of interaction between the two as follows:

> The patient transfers his concern to us through his transference

> We transfer our answer to the patient through our countertransference.

The definitions of both terms have changed considerably over time but right from the beginning there was and is something deeply revolutionary in their range and consistency, i.e. the determination to become more professional and develop a technology for a concern that is easy to formulate, but difficult to implement and has an existential impact on many areas of life:

How do I respect the other person?

Not just anyone, but precisely this particular person sitting in front of us as a very real being with the same existential questions.

In retrospect, the story that began with considering countertransference as a revolution appears as the story of respect and unconditional appreciation for the inevitably real in the other, also for the demonic, the shadow, the destructiveness.
The limited empathy that excluded the demonic became surmountable, expandable to what was previously excluded and disassociated. (...)

Literature on the lecture held on October 24, 2001:

Gill, M. M. (1996). *Die Übertragungsanalyse.* Frankfurt am Main: Fischer Taschenbuch Verlag.
König, K. (1998). *Gegenübertragungsanalyse.* Vandenhoeck & Ruprecht.
Racker, H. (1997). *Übertragung und Gegenübertragung.* (5th edition). Munich/Basel: Ernst Reinhardt Verlag.

Expansion, supplementation and further work for persons in charge in all fields of activity

Joerg Marxen offers individual sessions and seminars in the fields of *coaching, supervision* and *training* to deal with questions concerning the development of value systems and organizations, typical conflicts and resources in the interaction between different value systems at individual and organizational level and how to handle these in a professional and mature manner.